Albert and Sarah Jane

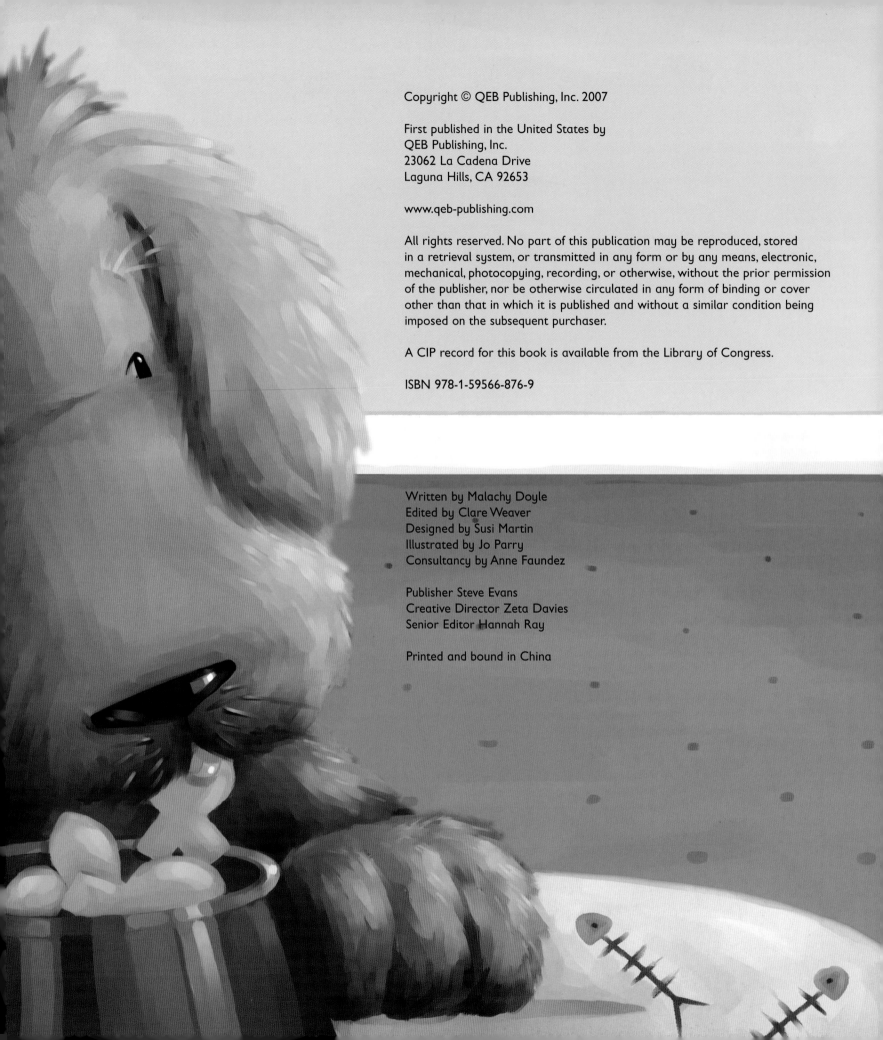

Copyright © QEB Publishing, Inc. 2007

First published in the United States by
QEB Publishing, Inc.
23062 La Cadena Drive
Laguna Hills, CA 92653

www.qeb-publishing.com

A CIP record for this book is available from the Library of Congress.

ISBN 978-1-59566-876-9

Written by Malachy Doyle
Edited by Clare Weaver
Designed by Susi Martin
Illustrated by Jo Parry
Consultancy by Anne Faundez

Publisher Steve Evans
Creative Director Zeta Davies
Senior Editor Hannah Ray

Printed and bound in China

Albert and Sarah Jane

Malachy Doyle

Illustrated by Jo Parry

QEB Publishing

Albert and Sarah Jane were the very best of friends. Their favorite thing to do was curl up in a great big cat-dog cuddle by the fire.

But there was one thing Albert liked even better than that.

And that was eating his yummy, scrummy crunchies from his big, blue bowl.

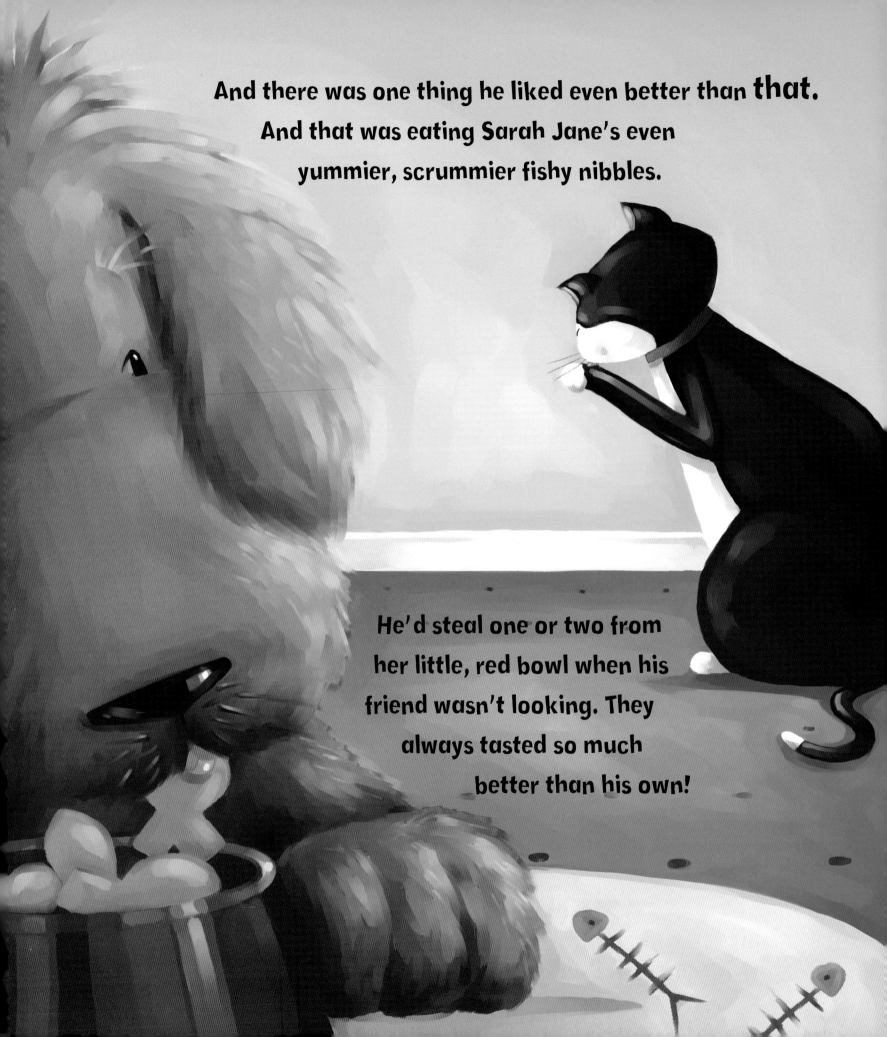

And there was one thing he liked even better than **that.**
And that was eating Sarah Jane's even
yummier, scrummier fishy nibbles.

He'd steal one or two from
her little, red bowl when his
friend wasn't looking. They
always tasted so much
better than his own!

But one morning, while Sarah Jane was out and about, Albert got a little carried away with his nibbling.

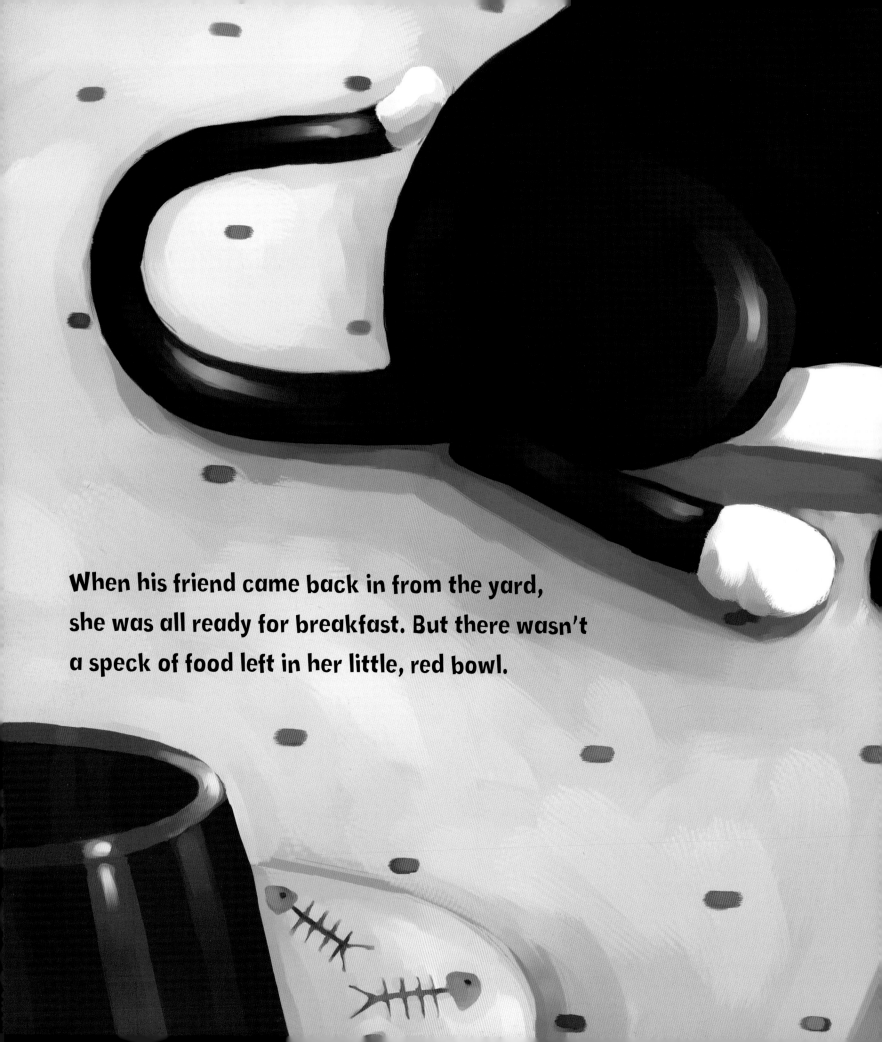

When his friend came back in from the yard,
she was all ready for breakfast. But there wasn't
a speck of food left in her little, red bowl.

When Sarah Jane looked to see if there was anything in Albert's big, blue bowl...

she found there wasn't a speck of food there, either!

She went to ask Albert why there wasn't any food to eat, but he was fast asleep in his basket.

That's odd, she thought, I'm sure he's fatter than usual. And I'm sure he smells all fishy, too!

"Okay," said Sarah Jane.
"I've had enough of this!"

She turned around and
marched straight
out of the house.

Albert opened one
eye and saw Sarah Jane
leaving through the pet door.

She'll be back, he thought.
She always comes back.

But Sarah Jane didn't come back.
She went to live next door, instead.

By that evening, Albert was lonely. By the next morning, he was howling at the pet door.

"Come home, Sarah Jane!" he cried.

Albert spotted Sarah Jane
through the upstairs window.

He smiled at her, in a doggy
sort of way, but Sarah Jane
ignored him.

So Albert sneaked out of the house, went next door, sat himself down on the doorstep, and howled.

"Come home, Sarah Jane!" he cried.

I miss you!

"Stop howling, you naughty dog!"
hissed Sarah Jane, coming down
to see what all the fuss was about.

"But I'm sad and lonely," said Albert.
"I want a great, big cat-dog cuddle by the fire."

"Well, the food's better over here and nobody steals it," said Sarah Jane.

"But it's lonely here, too, without a big, smelly lump of a dog to snuggle up to..."

"Me?" asked Albert.

"Yes, you," said Sarah Jane.

"Do you miss me, too?" asked Albert.

"I do," said Sarah Jane.

"Well...I'm sorry," said Albert.

"What for?" asked Sarah Jane.

"For gobbling up all your fishy nibbles," said Albert.

"Will you do it again?" asked Sarah Jane.

"I won't," said Albert.

"Will you even nibble them?" asked Sarah Jane.

"I won't," said Albert.

"Good," said Sarah Jane.

So she marched back home.
And Albert marched back
home behind her.

They had a little nibble
from their red and
blue bowls...

And then they curled up together in a great, big
cat-dog cuddle by the fire and fell asleep.

Notes for Teachers and Parents

- Have the children make a list of their classmate's cats and dogs. How many names can be used for people, too?

- Ask the children to make up six dog names and six cat names. Which are the favorites?

- Have the children make a pile of pretend yummy, scrummy crunchies from rolled-up scraps of paper. Make a pile of pretend fishy nibbles from cardboard cut into the shape of fish. Then get two bowls. In pairs, the children pretend to be either Albert or Sarah Jane. They take turns throwing their food into the bowls. The child who gets the most food in the bowls is the winner.

- Discuss the following questions: Why did Albert want to eat Sarah Jane's food? How would you describe him and the way in which he acted?

- Do the children think that Albert was really asleep when Sarah Jane came in to confront him? Have they ever pretended they were asleep when they weren't? Why?

- Ask the children if they think Sarah Jane was right to go live next door.

- Have the children act out the story as a play. One child takes the role of Sarah Jane and the other plays the role of Albert. Encourage the children to sound and move like a dog or cat. Afterward, discuss how it felt to be one of the characters. Then reverse the roles.

- Tell the story from Albert's point of view. For example, you could begin, "Hello. My name is Albert and I'm a dog." The children can join in and contribute to the story as it progresses.

- Then tell the story from Sarah Jane's point of view.

- Ask the children if they think Albert had changed by the end of the story. If so, why did he change?

- Ask the children if they have ever taken something that belonged to someone else. Why? What happened?

- Ask the children if they have ever taken something that belonged to a friend. What happened? How did the friend feel?

- Ask the children if they have ever had a falling out with a friend. What happened? How did they feel? Did they become friends again? Did they apologize? Do they find it hard to say sorry?

- Make a set of letter cards using the letters from the names "Albert" and "Sarah Jane." Mix up the "Albert" cards and see how many different words the children can make. Do the same with the "Sarah Jane" cards. Then put all the cards together and see how many words the children can make.